# Virtual Reality in the Courtroom

## Courtroom

### *Legal Visualization and Future of Trials*

# Table of Contents

# Chapter 1. Introduction

Welcome to an eye-opening exploration into the future of litigation in our splendid Special Report: "Virtual Reality in the Courtroom: Legal Visualization and Future of Trials". As courtroom drama embarks on a thrilling new trajectory, the way trials are conducted and perceived is on the cusp of a revolution, all thanks to cutting-edge technology. Straddling the line between reality and virtual realms, this vibrant report doesn't simply delve into the potential of legal visualization - it invites you along for a riveting, joyous journey. Brimming with engaging anecdotes, expert insights, and forecasts, and delivered in an inviting, easy-to-grasp language, this report promises to be a bright beacon for anyone interested in the intersection of law and technology. Allow yourself to be captivated by the spectacle of trials of the future - and who knows, you may just find yourself inspired to not merely witness, but shape the course of this gripping saga.

# Chapter 2. The Intersection of Law and Virtual Reality

Historically, legal proceedings have relied heavily on spoken testimony, physical evidence, and written documents. In an increasingly digital age, however, the courtrooms of the future might look very different. Virtual Reality (VR) technology, the immersive experience that allows individuals to interact within a simulated or real environment, offers exciting possibilities for visualizing scenarios in legal cases. These illustrate not just the transformations but the experiential shift we are witnessing in court proceedings.

## 2.1. The VR Transformation in Legal Procedures

Virtual Reality is set to play a significant role in improving legal procedures, from crime scene recreation to explaining complex topics in court. It allows for a three-dimensional, interactive display of evidence that was otherwise traditionally presented as static images or verbal descriptions. Facilitating a more comprehensive understanding of a situation, it could potentially result in more accurate verdicts and improve the overall justice system.

An initial area of impact is the use of VR in enabling crime scene re-enactment. Often, such spatial environments can be challenging to understand based only on photographs or verbal descriptions. VR has the potential to offer juries a virtual tour, enabling them to comprehend the implication of objects' positioning, distances, or the functionality of the entire locale. With greater understanding comes increased chance of arriving at a just outcome.

Another aspect being transformed by VR is the training of law enforcement officials and first responders. Incident scene preservation is crucial in investigations and subsequent judicial proceedings. VR can provide inexperienced officers with virtually simulated environments to practice handling evidence and responding to situations, helping to reduce errors in real incidents.

## 2.2. Challenges and Pitfalls of VR Adoption

With all new technological advances, however, come challenges and potential pitfalls. One concern is the potential for prejudice or bias to be introduced through manipulated imagery or dramatization. Standards would need to be established to prevent such misuse and to ensure a fair trial. Ethical considerations also arise in exposing jury members to potentially disturbing content without proper psychological support.

Additionally, issues arise regarding digital recreations' accuracy, particularly when concerning older crimes or incidents. Understanding changes in an environment over time can be critical in assessing a scenario accurately. However, recreating an older environment in VR could involve a certain degree of estimation or assumptions, potentially leading to inaccuracies.

## 2.3. The Influence of VR on Litigation and Arbitration

Beyond the courtroom, VR is likely to influence litigation and arbitration effectively. It could be used in a variety of ways, such as creating reconstructions of accidents for personal injury claims or property disputes. Architectural and engineering concepts which could be challenging to explain verbally or through diagrams, might become more tangible when presented in a three-dimensional and interactive setting.

A significant area where VR could be influential is in arbitration, particularly regarding international business disputes. These disputes often involve complex technical or financial matters that may be difficult to understand. Being able to virtually present data in a simplified, coherent, and engaging manner might help facilitate better understanding, enabling more straightforward discussion and resolution.

## 2.4. Legal Implications and Regulations

As VR reshapes legal procedures, it will necessitate the review of existing laws and regulations and quite possibly, the creation of new ones. The admissibility of virtual reality evidence, the accuracy and authenticity of VR simulations, and potential impacts on jury decisions will be new legal landscapes that need exploration. Regulatory bodies will have to devise ways to harness the benefits while mitigating the risks, facilitating fair trials while ensuring the technology is not misused.

As we stand on the brink of a seismic shift in legal technology, it is not only about embracing change - it involves understanding the implications, preparing for challenges, and building an improved justice system. It is a captivating journey, with virtual reality leading the way, turning fantasy into reality, bringing abstract to tangible, and providing tools for improved accessibility and understanding in court proceedings.

## 2.5. The Bygone Arena and the Road Ahead

A glance at courtrooms' history reveals a journey from the spoken word to the written document, then to photographs, and now to the virtual replication of reality. The power of VR in a courtroom isn't simply its technological prowess; it's the ability to translate some of the most challenging and complex aspects of law into something interactive and visual, bridging understanding gaps along the way.

Virtual reality is promising yet unchartered terrain for legal processes. As VR becomes more prevalent, and as courtrooms become comfortable with this new frontier, the legal system may see an era where cases become more about precise visualization than imaginative interpretations. An exciting future awaits at the intersection of law and virtual reality - a future that stands to redefine legal norms, pushing boundaries and opening new avenues for justice!

# Chapter 3. The Advent of Legal Visualization

The concept of legal visualization is not entirely new. For centuries, legal professionals have used various types of visualization to highlight critical aspects of their arguments - from drawings and diagrams to photos and video recordings. Slowly but surely, more sophisticated methods of legal visualization have begun to permeate courtrooms, influencing nearly every facet of the trial process, from initial investigation to verdict delivery.

## 3.1. The Evolution of Legal Visualization

Even in the most loquacious of judgment texts, the adage "A picture is worth a thousand words" holds. Visualization has always played a crucial role in judicial proceedings. It began with simple sketches completed by court artists and has evolved to photographs, videos, and, more recently, digital exhibits.

With the advent of computers and then internet technology, courts began to explore the possibilities of digital visualization - slide shows, animations, and other forms of digital exhibits became more commonplace in the courtroom. These tools improved the comprehension of complex issues and enabled juries to visualize scenarios more effectively than oral testimony alone.

## 3.2. The Breakthroughs in Technology

The 21st century has seen cutting-edge technologies emerge that can be harnessed for legal visualization, and chief among them is virtual reality (VR). Now, eyewitness accounts can be supplemented or, in some cases, replaced by 3D simulations of crime scenes or events that are true to scale and offer a real-world perspective that was previously not possible to achieve. These simulated environments aren't bound by static observations. Instead, they offer a 360-degree panoramic view that allows juries to explore scenarios at their own pace.

Another technology aiding in the shift toward visual litigation is augmented reality (AR), which overlays computer-generated images on a user's view of the real world, thus providing a composite view. This technology provides a unique angle not only to the way evidence is presented but also how juries perceive it. Imagine being able to interact with a crime scene without actually being there, interface with pieces of evidence, and witness events unfold right before your eyes – these are the possibilities that AR brings to the table.

A third, often overlooked, technology in this mix is artificial intelligence (AI). AI can assist in visualizing patterns within complex datasets or simplifying piles of documents into easy-to-understand visual models, thus aiding lawyers and investigators in their pursuit of justice.

# 3.3. Standards and Protocols for Legal Visualization

One of the challenges with using these new tools in a legal setting is the lack of standardized rules and norms that govern their use. Given how new this technology is in the legal field, there isn't a widely recognized protocol that legal professionals can follow. This means that while the opportunities for using VR, AR, and AI for visual litigation are exciting, they're also subject to a high degree of scrutiny.

Evidence presented in court must be reliable and verifiable for it to hold weight. With the increased use of these detailed simulations, it may be challenging to ensure that the recreated scenarios accurately represent the real-world events they're meant to depict.

This presents a significant need for a universal standard that can assure the objectivity and accuracy of VR, AR, and AI evidence. It's extraordinarily vital to establish a legal framework to help translate, validate, and standardize these new forms of evidence, ensuring their credibility and reliability equal to that of traditional forms of evidence.

# 3.4. The Future of Legal Visualization

The future of legal visualization is as thrilling as it is uncertain, bound by the progress of technology and the evolution of legal norms. If we can efficiently address the issues surrounding validity and objectivity, these new forms of visualization can bring tremendous value to the legal process. Imagine law enforcement officers using VR during the investigation process, lawyers using AR to recount events to a jury, or judges using AI insights to deliver fair and unbiased verdicts.

The opportunities are endless, and they fundamentally challenge our traditional view of the courtroom. This chapter paints a picture of a future that's not too far off, a future where these types of technological advancements aren't just novel enhancements to what's already there, but fully integrated components of the legal system itself.

With the seriousness of the justice system and the lives and freedoms often at stake, it's essential to ensure that we're creating a system that uses these advancements properly while maintaining a high standard of fairness and objectivity. And so, as we journey into this brave, new, virtual world, it's essential to keep the legal scales balanced to ensure that while the methods may change, the service of justice never wavers.

# Chapter 4. Barriers and Breakthroughs in VR Technology

At the core of understanding any novel technology is recognizing that it not only heralds breakthroughs but also grapples with barriers. As we boldly tread the path towards embedding Virtual Reality (VR) in legal spaces, it becomes imperative to conduct a meticulous examination of both aspects. This chapter will critically analyze the current impediments faced by VR, its evolving nature, the precipice of breakthroughs, and the potential implications for our legal systems.

## 4.1. Technological Limitations

Despite the rapid pace of technological advancement, VR still faces significant constraints limiting its broader application. VR headsets currently dominate the market, but their adoption has been stunted by issues like functional incompatibility, expensive hardware, and a high degree of technical know-how required for their operation. Another deterrent is 'cybersickness', a side effect for some users who struggle with its immersive nature, leading to nausea and discomfort.

Developing VR applications specific to showcasing complex legal procedures or presentations also poses challenges. Programmatically replicating the intricacies of dynamic human interaction remains a formidable task. Achieving seamless and realistic portrayals is fraught with difficulties, mainly due to the subtleties of human communication, such as micro-expressions, postures, and voice modulations. Such limitations hold VR back from realizing its complete impact in the courtroom.

## 4.2. Data Privacy and Security Concerns

The huge datasets involved in VR simulations prompt privacy and security quandaries. Unauthorized access to sensitive data can lead to its misuse, potentially affecting trial outcomes. Conflicts may arise between maintaining judicial transparency and upholding the confidentiality of the parties involved.

## 4.3. Legal and Regulatory Hurdles

While VR holds promise for revolutionizing legal proceedings, it remains in limbo when it comes to statutory regulations. Wide acceptance of VR in the legal landscape requires modifications to existing laws, propelled by precisely defining its legal status and potential implications.

## 4.4. Accessibility and Participation

Not all potential users of legal VR can afford the requisite infrastructure, raising concerns about access to justice. Moreover, while VR could potentially democratize the courtroom space, it also exposes socio-technological divides. Ensuring equal participation from individuals of varying technological prowess is critical to prevent bias in VR-facilitated legal proceedings.

## 4.5. Forging Ahead: Computational Improvements

The paradox of barriers often catalyzes path-breaking work, and this holds true in surmounting VR's technological hurdles as well. Major tech players are pushing at the boundaries of hardware and software capabilities, aiming at more user-friendly VR interfaces. Progress in GPU technology, eye-tracking, haptic feedback and around reduction of latency rates and screen-door effects are all positive signs on the horizon.

## 4.6. Better Software, Greater Realism

Graphically realistic software developments are transforming once implausible virtual environments into believable realities. Increasingly sophisticated 3D modeling software and physics engines are paving the way for higher fidelity simulations. Moreover, advancements in artificial intelligence and machine learning are inching closer to reproducing nuanced human behaviors.

## 4.7. Addressing Data Privacy and Security Concerns

Data encryption has become a norm, with developers deploying advanced cryptographic methods to secure sensitive VR data. Multi-factor authentication and precise access controls are complementing these efforts. However, pivotal developments are anticipated in areas like blockchain, decentralization, and federated learning to yield secure, enhanced VR experiences.

## 4.8. Legal Frameworks Evolving

The legal field is slowly adapting and clarifying VR's place within its frameworks. New laws conceived in consultation with VR experts aim at protecting users' rights and regulate VR implementation in legal processes.

## 4.9. A Global Digital Divide - An Opportunity for Unity

Efforts are underway to broaden access to VR technology globally. Strategies such as promoting affordable VR tools, strengthening digital infrastructure, and offering training programs can prove effective in closing the technical skill gap and ensure fair participation, thereby aiding the global democratization of justice.

## 4.10. Lifelike Avatars – A Journey Ahead

Technological innovations are making strides towards creating lifelike avatars. This evolution is crucial in the context of courtrooms of the future, where achieving more realistic digital representations leads to fruitful, unbiased discussions and judgments.

The pilgrimage towards a VR-enabled legal system is likely to be tumultuous and intriguing. As we maneuver through the labyrinth of barriers, each breakthrough takes us one step closer to a future where justice isn't confined to the physical limitations of a courtroom but is instead a truly immersive, inclusive, and global phenomenon. The onus falls on us, pioneers of this change, to be vigilant, patient, and persistent, ensuring the nascent promise of VR in courtrooms doesn't fade into obscurity, but rather illuminates a captivating new era in legal history.

# Chapter 5. Case Studies: Virtual Reality in Current Trials

Teetering on the cusp of experiential technology, the realm of law has begun to incorporate virtual reality (VR) as a method to enhance courtroom proceedings. This emerging trend has opened avenues for a more effective representation of case facts and contexts, enabling a more comprehensive understanding for juries, and ultimately, influencing the judgement of a case. The following case studies provide deep explorations into how virtual reality is being incorporated into the legal landscape.

## 5.1. The Californian Murder Mystery

In a California murder case, investigators embraced the power of VR to walk jurors through the crime scene, a precedent-setting move that marked a significant shift in how evidence was traditionally presented. The victim, found dead in his San Francisco apartment, had minimal signs of struggle, making the crime hard for investigators to solve using traditional methods and making the narrative difficult to convey to the jury.

A virtual simulation was created using the thousands of digital photographs taken by the forensic team. The objective was to enable the jury to virtually walk through the crime scene and observe the arrangement, helping them better understand the probable sequence of events. With the VR headsets on, jurors gained a transformative perspective, aiding them in understanding fine-grained details that helped guide their verdict.

This case marks an important milestone in the application of VR technology in legal scenarios, as it showed how the technology could afford an immersive and interactive investigation experience, where ambiguity could be minimized.

# 5.2. Tracing the Car Crash

In another case, a road traffic accident that occurred on a chaotic intersection was disputed over who was at fault. The traditional 2D satellite images, street, and cockpit views captured by cameras failed to provide a clear view of the sequence of events.

An innovative legal tech firm was engaged to create a three-dimensional simulation of the intersection. With the use of VR, the jury was presented with a walkthrough of the events leading up to the accident from various angles - the drivers' perspectives, pedestrians, and even from an overhead drone view. The VR experience provided a holistic understanding of the environmental conditions, traffic dynamics, and the drivers' possible viewpoints at the time of the accident, which significantly influenced the jury's understanding and decision-making process.

# 5.3. The Sexual Harassment Allegation

While the power of VR has been harnessed predominantly in criminal litigation, its potential in civil matters is also prominent. In a sexual harassment case, the plaintiff faced considerable challenges in effectively communicating the gravity of her experiences due to the highly subjective nature of such claims.

A VR scenario, replicating the working environment and the specific instances of harassment, was developed based on the plaintiff's account. This allowed court participants to experience the harassment from the victim's perspective, facilitating a more empathetic understanding of the incident. The case, while not publicized due to its sensitive nature, underscored the potential of VR in creating emotionally immersive experiences and its utility in tackling complex socio-legal issues.

# 5.4. Archaeological Litigation & Cultural Heritage

In an unprecedented development, attorneys leveraging VR got involved in archaeological litigation, largely revolving around cultural heritage disputes. The intricacies associated with the historic and archaeological context render these cases complex, with exhaustive documentary evidence equally perplexing for jurors.

In one such culturally charged litigation, VR was utilized to recreate the archaeological site in question – letting jurors explore it in its original glory. This step offered a more encompassing and true-to-life understanding of the site, facilitating an impactful connection and insightful deliberations around its cultural significance.

These aforementioned cases beautifully illustrate how VR has started to reshape the course of legal exploration and judgement. Although the technology is not widespread yet, the altering landscape of the courtrooms and the increasingly conclusive verdicts document the potential of VR to be a game-changing tool in legal and courtroom scenarios. As this technology further penetrates the judicial system, we can anticipate a future where the ambiguity of the courtroom will significantly be reduced, improving the efficiency and effectiveness of the legal processes.

# Chapter 6. The Legal Profession in the VR Age

The implications of VR for the legal profession have been wide and varied. With its potential to recreate scenes, provide immersive experiences, and convey complex ideas easily, VR is becoming a stalwart tool for lawyers, judges, and the broader court staff.

## 6.1. Roles and Repercussions: Legal Practitioners and VR

Legal practitioners have to keep abreast of technological advances to maintain their efficacy in court. The dawn of VR has presented new opportunities and hurdles which they have to grasp and grapple with, respectively. Foremost among these challenges is understanding and exploiting the technology itself. VR systems and software represent an entirely new medium for lawyers. It's mandatory for them to learn the functioning, capabilities, and limitations of these systems. Not only that, but attorneys must also know when it is appropriate and effective to use VR and when it is not.

On the other hand, purchasing and maintaining VR technology can be a logistical and financial burden for law firms, particularly smaller ones. However, as VR technology becomes more widespread and the costs decrease, it's likely that this hurdle will be ameliorated.

## 6.2. Understanding and Interacting with VR Evidence

Understanding VR is one facet of the issue - interacting with it is another. Lawyers regularly deal with pieces of evidence that form the cornerstone of their cases. As VR becomes more incorporated into court proceedings, lawyers will increasingly encounter VR evidence. Attorneys must be comfortable with VR platforms and know how to use the evidence to their advantage. This might involve navigating through a VR scene, adjusting the VR environment, or even elucidating evidence in a virtual setting.

Underpinning this is the issue of authenticity. In the same way that photoshopped images can present a misleading view of events, VR renderings, too, have to be examined judiciously. Lawyers will need to work hand in hand with technology experts to authenticate VR evidence.

# 6.3. Ethical Dilemmas & New Rules in VR litigation

As legal practitioners leapfrog into the virtual world, they tumble into a new realm of ethical dilemmas and regulatory hurdles. Lawyers would have to navigate these novel situations while upholding the ethical codes that underpin the legal profession.

For example, what if a lawyer uses VR to reconstruct a crime scene but intentionally leaves out or alters some elements? Or what if a VR presentation is so emotionally compelling that it sways the jury beyond reason?

To prevent such ethical breaches, clear guidelines would need to be formulated. Lawyers, judges, and regulating bodies would have to work together to establish these guidelines, enforce their implementation, and assess their effectiveness.

## 6.4. The Brave New World: Bench and Bar in the VR Age

The reverberations of the VR revolution wouldn't be confined to the legal practitioners donning the headsets - they would echo across the courtroom, influencing judges, witnesses, and the jury.

For courtroom judges, who are often gatekeepers to the admission of evidence, the task of assessing VR evidence would be a new challenge. They would be called upon to answer whether VR evidence is reliable, whether it might unduly influence the jury, or if its introduction constitutes a violation of the defendant's rights.

However, VR wouldn't be an entirely disruptive force. Indeed, we can envision cases where VR technology aids and aligns with legal principles. For example, in cases where the best evidence rule applies, VR reconstructions might be admitted as superior evidence if they precisely and accurately recreate a scene using data and algorithms.

## 6.5. Training the Lawyers of tomorrow

To prepare today's lawyers for tomorrow's VR courtroom, law schools and educational institutions will need to align their offerings with emerging technology. VR training could form part of the curriculum, equipping law learners with the requisite knowledge and skills.

In addition, law schools could employ VR in moot courts, making them more immersive and dynamic. Instead of remaining confined to books and blackboards, law education could morph into something akin to a realistic rehearsal of courtroom proceedings - transitions enabled by VR technology.

The judicial galaxy, traditionally averse to abrupt changes, stands on the precipice of a VR revolution. From attorneys to judges, and from witnesses to defendants, everyone in the courtroom will feel the ripples caused by this metamorphosis. These changes pose both opportunities and challenges, demanding adaptability and foresight from all stakeholders. However, one thing is certain - the VR tide is surging, and it promises to reshape the contours of the courtroom landscape forever.

# Chapter 7. Potential Risks and Ethical Challenges

As we dare to dream of a future where virtual reality (VR) is integrated into our courtrooms, it is incumbent upon us to assess the potential risks and ethical challenges that may come hand in hand with such technological advancements. Appreciating these concerns will not only guarantee that technology serves the justice system justly, but will also be pivotal in shaping policy guidelines and legal frameworks suitable for an era of virtual trials.

## 7.1. Impact on Human Interaction

Typically, a courtroom is a place charged with emotion, where human interaction plays a critical part in decision-making processes. The shift to virtual reality might render the emotive component of legal proceedings sterile, potentially robbing them of an essential, human angle.

For one, the digital divide could escalate in a VR courtroom. People who are not technologically adept could be placed at a disadvantage, unable to fully grasp or participate in proceedings shown through a VR headset. Furthermore, potential malfunctions of VR equipment, or poorly designed software, may skew the experience, potentially leading to an unjust outcome.

## 7.2. Confidentiality and Privacy

Confidentiality is fundamental to the justice system. However, the transition to a virtual environment could compromise confidentiality due to potential security vulnerabilities. Breaches of privacy could occur either at the point of virtual data creation, transmission, or storage.

Moreover, there might be questions regarding consent when it comes to recording and storing personal data in VR trials. For instance, the representation of individuals digitally could lead to potential misuse or unethical behavior, in some instances even leading to the virtual portrayal of individuals without their approval.

## 7.3. Authenticity and Manipulation of VR Representations

Virtual reality thrives on recreating reality, but this could lead to potential misinformation or manipulation of facts. It's crucial that the VR representations are authentic and true to the events they reinstate. Unethical manipulations of VR environments might lead to wrongful judgments.

VR developers, in particular, could inadvertently introduce bias into their recreations. Since VR scenarios are necessarily reductive, leaving out certain elements or emphasizing others based on the developers' decisions, there's the risk of omitting something crucial from the virtual narrative.

## 7.4. Accessibility and Equality in Law

The incorporation of VR into legal proceedings carries the risk of creating a new digital divide, affecting the very principles of access to justice. The costs related to the adoption of VR, from the technology itself to the required human resources and the necessary training, may place a substantial burden on smaller agencies and individuals.

It's important to ensure that access to justice isn't made conditional on the ability to engage with advanced technologies or on the financial capacity to access these technologies. Regulators and policy-makers need to evaluate carefully these potential pitfalls in the widespread adoption of VR in courtrooms.

# 7.5. Accountability and Liability

Determining responsibility for VR-related mishaps could be challenging, as the technology potentially implicates multiple stakeholders, from device manufacturers and software developers to court administrators. All share responsibility in ensuring a fair and error-free process.

In conclusion, the use of virtual reality in courtrooms indeed promises to revolutionize the legal landscape. However, such benefits come with potential risks and ethical challenges that need to be mitigated against with caution.

As we progress, it's fundamental that we foster an inclusive discussion involving technologists, legal practitioners, policy-makers, and society at large to ensure the technology is adopted responsibly. It is only through a collective effort that we can make VR courtrooms the harbingers of justice they're meant to be, and not catalysts for legal disarray. A future with VR courtrooms isn't just about staying ahead of the technology curve; it's about ensuring those advancements serve us all justly.

# Chapter 8. Transforming Juror Experience with VR

There's no doubt that the juror's role in a trial is a critical one. Responsible for determining the truth based on the evidence presented, they are essentially the eyes and ears of the court. This pivotal role has traditionally relied heavily on oral presentations and still images. However, with the advancements in virtual reality (VR) technologies, the juror experience is set to be transformed, offering new ways of presenting evidence, reconstructing scenes, and visualizing hypothetical scenarios.

## 8.1. The Advent of VR in Law

The legal field has always been adaptive to technology, often embracing advancements that help in the pursuit of justice. Virtual reality (VR), as a digital tool, is no exception. Essentially a simulated experience that can mimic or surpass the real world, VR can facilitate sensory experiences, such as sights, sounds, and in some cases, touch.

But how does VR apply in a courtroom setting? The answer lies in the power of visualization. VR can take a juror beyond the abstract notions and convoluted details of a case, allowing them to become a part of a realistic, immersive reenactment of an event.

## 8.2. VR for Visualizing Facts

Consider a crime scene that has been recreated in VR. Instead of relying on verbal descriptions, dated photographs or poorly-drawn sketches, a juror can put on VR goggles and find themselves standing at the scene. They can examine the distances between objects, observe things from different perspectives, and potentially gain an understanding that flat exhibits could never convey.

As virtual reality develops, it also has the potential to incorporate haptic feedback, giving jurors a real 'feel' of the evidence. Imagine feeling the weight of a weapon or the rough texture of a piece of evidence in a crime. It is the closest one can get to 'being there', without actually having been present at the scene of the crime.

# 8.3. Case Reenactments and Scenario Simulations

The beauty of VR lies in not just the ability to reconstruct scenes, but also recreate events. Jurors can observe a virtual reenactment of the crime based on the evidence and testimonies collected.

Moreover, VR can be used to simulate different scenarios as per the arguments of the prosecution and defense. For instance, in a case involving a vehicle accident, VR could be used to demonstrate what each driver could see in the moments leading up to the collision.

# 8.4. Addressing the Concerns

Despite its promise, introducing VR into the courtroom is not without challenges. There are legal, ethical, and practical concerns that need addressing.

Creating a believable VR experience for court use is an expensive and time-consuming process. Not all courts may have the resources to implement such technology. There is also the question of building a universally accepted protocol or standard for creating and examining VR evidence, given its complex nature.

Moreover, the accuracy of VR simulations can be hotly contested in court, as they are ultimately based on someone's interpretation of the scene or event.

There are also ethical concerns, such as the risk of emotional manipulation. VR is known to invoke strong emotional responses. If used recklessly, it can unfairly sway the perceptions of the jurors.

# 8.5. Looking Towards the Future

As we grapple with these current concerns, we also look to a future where VR becomes a common tool in a legal setting. As technology advances and becomes more accessible, the use of VR to aid juries can potentially standardize, transform, and perhaps even expedite trial proceedings.

The possibilities offered by VR are staggering in their scope. As virtual reality becomes more sophisticated, we may soon see real-time recreations, interactive exhibits, experiential testimonies, and much more.

The future of juries and trials will be dynamic, as VR technologies permeate courtrooms. We stand on the brink of what may very well be a revolution in legal proceedings. It is a thrilling, challenging journey that will shape not just the juror experience, but the entirety of trial proceedings. Time will indeed tell if the scales of justice will tip favorably in the face of this technological leap.

# Chapter 9. Impact on Evidence Presentation

The traditional courtroom has always faced acute challenges in the presentation and comprehension of evidence, especially when dealing with complex cases involving medical malpractice, intricate finances, or technical scientific data. However, through transformative virtual reality (VR) technologies, we are beginning to witness the dawn of a new era that aims to overcome these hurdles with immersive, detailed, and accurate visualizations.

## 9.1. The Evidential Revolution Brought by VR

In a world where "seeing is believing," evidence presented via VR provides an unparalleled edge. Commonly referred to as 'Legal Visualization,' VR technology has tremendous potential to present evidence in a comprehensive, absorbing manner that aids understanding and aids retention.

When jurors or arbitrators can 'see' the evidence with their own eyes - walk through a virtual crime scene, experience a simulation of an accident, or visualize complex financial transactions - it provides a level of engagement and comprehension hitherto unattainable.

## 9.2. VR Simulated Crime Scenes

Consider a murder trial, where the crime scene can be recreated meticulously within a VR environment. With VR headsets, jurors can explore the scene themselves, pick up virtual objects, review points of entry or egress without any external influence, providing them with a more comprehensive understanding about what could have happened.

Furthermore, VR allows for simultaneous viewing by all parties involved, eliminating the need for multiple site visits, and creating a shared experience that lends to more informed deliberations.

# 9.3. Reenactments and Simulations

Other visualization techniques include the recreation of events, such as car accidents or medical procedures, that could have led to a lawsuit. VR technology can simulate these events in an authentic, interactive way, allowing the juror to virtually step into the shoes of any party involved, be it the plaintiff, defendant, or a third-party witness.

Imagine the ability to experience a surgeon's viewpoint during a complex medical procedure gone awry, or a simultaneous view of both drivers during a vehicular accident – the understanding it can provide is unmatched by any other form of evidence presentation.

# 9.4. Visualizing Abstract Concepts

In certain cases, evidence might need to speak on abstract concepts or complex processes, such as the working of a specific machine, cyber attacks, algorithm-based decision making, or financial sophistication.

Often, the oral and written presentation of these concepts fall short, primarily due to their inherent complexity. VR can provide a visual walkthrough of these processes, making them easily comprehensible. For instance, during a patent dispute over a highly technical product, VR can give jurors a tangible experience of the product's functioning, aiding their understanding exponentially.

## 9.5. Data Visualization

Virtual Reality can also be employed efficiently for the visualization and interpretation of massive data-centric evidence, which often becomes mind-numbing and challenging to comprehend when presented traditionally.

By transforming mundane spreadsheets and reports into impressive and simplified 3D graphics, multidimensional data can be easily absorbed. For example, tracking fraudulent activities in a huge pile of transactions could be accurately and swiftly performed in a VR environment.

## 9.6. Caveats and Challenges

Despite its many advantages, introducing VR into the courtroom is not without its challenges. Primarily, the potential for manipulation is a concern: how do we ensure that the VR representations are an accurate depiction of reality and not some form of an enhanced, skewed, or downplayed version of events?

There's also the fear that the immersive nature of VR could play on the emotional biases of the jurors, inaccurately swaying their decisions. The novelty of the experience might also form a bias, as jurors could give undue preference to VR-presented evidence over traditional forms.

Additionally, there's the question of accessibility and consistency. Can all courtrooms afford VR technology, or will its use lead to a disparity in legal proceedings across jurisdictions?

## 9.7. Looking Ahead

Despite these challenges, there's an unequivocal agreement among experts that VR will shape the future of evidence presentation, bringing revolutionizing changes to the legal landscape. The testimony of 'virtual witnesses', digital forensics, holographic evidence are all on the horizon, as sci-fi as they might sound.

The bridge from 'hearsay' to 'see-say,' as many proponents love to refer it, is expected to amplify not only the extent of understanding but also the fairness and efficiency of trials. As legal practitioners, technology providers, and regulators steer through the various challenges, it is certain that VR, in all its immersive glory, will find its rightful place in the courtroom of the future.

As VR continues to evolve, refine, and integrate into our everyday lives, it's imperative that the legal world keeps pace. Equally crucial is the need for well-drafted guidelines and regulations ensuring the ethical use of such technology.

In conclusion, Virtual Reality has already extended its foot in the door of the legal space, ushering an exciting chapter of innovation and transformation. The impact on evidence presentation is likely to be profound and an area that all legal professionals should keenly observe and prepare for. Several hurdles remain, but the efforts to further this technology could herald a significant leap forward in the administration of justice.

# Chapter 10. The Future of Law Practice: Predictions and Possibilities

The digital transformation that has been disrupting numerous traditional industries is no longer knocking at the doorstep of legal profession. It is here, transforming the very fabric of how legal matters are addressed, and shaking the solid ground that the millennia-old profession has stood on to its core.

## 10.1. The Age of Digital Transformation

Technology impacts various aspects of traditional legal practice, restructuring the idea of legal proceedings and lawyering. AI, blockchain, virtual reality, and other burgeoning technologies have started to demonstrate their transformative potential in several areas of law.

One profound wave of change looming over the legal landscape is virtual reality (VR). At this fascinating intersection of law and technology, VR is primed to redefine the legal profession as we know it. From crime scene recreation and virtual juries, to lawyer training and beyond, VR is carving a space for itself within an industry which is traditionally known for its preference for the status quo.

## 10.2. Virtual Reality in Legal Education and Training

Lawyer training and jurisprudence could greatly benefit from embracing VR technologies. Virtual reality learning environments can offer an immersive, interactive experience for aspiring lawyers. Realistic courtroom simulations can provide invaluable practice without the high stakes of an actual court trial.

In this scenario-based training, everything is conceivable. Trainees could explore a virtual crime scene, practicing important observational skills and using critical thinking to piece together events. They may also participate in a virtual deposition, honing their questioning abilities or responding techniques in realistic situations.

These possibilities extend beyond mere practice as well. A fully immersive VR experience can provide legal professionals with a chance to explore the impact of their decisions from all angles. One could see the consequences of legal rulings years down the line, without actually having to wait for the repercussions to transpire.

# 10.3. The Evolution of Courtrooms

Another domain poised for digital revolution is the actual courtroom. The technology to create lifelike 3D recreations of crime scenes or events related to cases is becoming increasingly affordable and accurate. This will very likely result in lawyers using VR to show, rather than tell, the story behind their cases.

Such use of VR may also expand the horizons of judges and juries. Instead of relying on the interpretations of the opposing counsels, juries may have the opportunity to independently investigate a matter or incident from their own perspectives, eliminating some level of bias in their verdicts.

Remote proceedings are another aspect to consider, especially with the global pandemic making the prospect of in-person trials riskier. A fully virtual court where all parties, from judge to attorneys to witnesses, are physically distant but virtually present, could mitigate risks while maintaining the decorum and seriousness of court proceedings.

# 10.4. The Blockchain Revolution

Parallel to virtual reality, blockchain technology also stands to drastically alter the future of law practice. While blockchain is commonly associated with cryptocurrencies such as Bitcoin, its applications are surprisingly varied and relevant to the legal domain. The ability to create smart contracts, for instance, could automate certain contractual obligations and transactions without the need for third parties.

Linked with this is the development of decentralized autonomous organizations (DAOs). Through blockchain and smart contract technology, DAOs are able to operate independently of human intervention, following preprogrammed rules to carry out tasks or make decisions. This has profound implications for legal understandings of responsibility and liability, challenging the very bedrock of governance and legal principles.

# 10.5. Lawyers' Roles in the Future

The legal profession itself is not immune from the transformation. Lawyers will have to adapt, not just in terms of how they operate, but in how they approach their roles. While traditionally esteemed for their knowledge of case laws and statutes, future lawyers will require different competencies. They'd need to understand how technology integrates into the existing legal landscape, how to use these tools to better serve their clients, and how to adapt to the rapidly shifting paradigms.

Another possibility is the increasing automation of certain aspects of legal work. To an extent, this future is already here. AI technologies can sift through mountains of legal documents for discovery or explore thousands of jurisprudence pages for case research, functions that were once handled by human lawyers. And while certain areas of law practice would still require the human touch -

such as courtroom advocacy, strategic negotiation, or client management - technology is challenging the traditional image of legal professionals.

In the longer term, it's conceivable that new specializations will emerge in the intersection of tech and law, such as VR law, AI ethics law, or blockchain legal experts. Professionals with technical know-how and understanding of legal jurisdictions will be sought after, marking a significant shift from traditional practices.

# 10.6. Conclusion: Embracing a New Legal Reality

The future of law practice, in many ways, mirrors the broader societal shift towards digital transformation. Technology will not merely modify current procedures; it promises to revolutionize the entire field, questioning long-standing principles and altering the very essence of legal practice. For those willing to adapt and evolve, this might well herald an era of faster, more accessible, and (perhaps) more impartial justice system. However, society must also stay vigilant against potential risks and drawbacks that will accompany these advancements.

If anything, navigating this upcoming digital revolution will demand not only technological acumen but a firm grounding in legal ethics, empathy, and critical thinking. The challenge lies not in mastering these digital tools but in ensuring they serve the wider societal imperative of justice.

# Chapter 11. Closing Arguments: The Long-term Implications of VR in Court

Legal scholars and tech enthusiasts alike have long been debating the potential pitfalls and rewards of implementing VR technology in organized courtrooms. The discourse around virtual reality (VR) in trials often presents VR as an astonishing tool capable of revolutionizing litigation. From recreating crime scenes to simulating a lawyer's perspective, the possibilities appear endless. However, it is crucial to consider the long-term implications.

===Understanding The Potential

Virtual Reality can vastly transform how we perceive and understand information in a courtroom. Imagine a case where a vehicle accident has occurred. Instead of relying on witness testimonies and analyst reports, the courtroom can use VR to recreate the scene. Everyone, from the jury, judge, lawyers, to spectators, can view what happened from different perspectives. The accident's details become much clearer this way than any verbal or written record could possibly illustrate.

That said, the use of VR in a courtroom stretches beyond just crime scene recreation. Namely, taking witness testimony. Witness reliability is often questionable due to factors like memory decay and emotional state, affecting their ability to recall events accurately. However, VR can considerably reduce reliance on witness testimony by providing an unbiased, precise view of the events in question.

However, with such sweeping changes, we must consider not only the transforming potential but also the associated risks and concerns, particularly those with long-term implications.

### ===Uncharted Territory: Ethical Consideration

Reshaping litigation using Virtual Reality comes bundled with a slew of ethical and fairness concerns. Chief among these concerns is objectivity versus subjectivity. VR exquisitely captures details, making them seem more real to someone who was not at the crime scene. It could potentially skew the perception of the viewer, making things appear a certain way which may not be entirely accurate. This augmented reality raises the question of "Memory Contamination" where the VR's recreation might overwrite or cloud participants' memories or impressions of the events.

Moreover, VR could unintentionally end up providing one side with an undue edge over the other, compromising the basic principle of giving each party an equal opportunity to present their case.

### ===Economic Implications

The economical perspective needs thorough consideration too. The cost of implementing a full VR system, which would include both hardware and trained professionals to operate it and interpret data, can be quite high. Currently, this technology is not widespread, thus putting smaller courts at a disadvantage due to limited resources.

This discrepancy in access would raise questions about the overall fairness of the legal process. After all, should justice depend on how technologically advanced a court is?

### ===Legal Framework Considerations

How will existing legal frameworks adapt to these technological advancements? New procedures will likely need to be established to ensure proper usage of the technology. For example, when and how should VR be used, and who will decide?

It's essential that policy-making bodies take these questions into account to ensure fair justice under this new system.

### Technological Sabotage: A New Front for Crimes?

With the rise of VR comes new avenues for criminal activity too. Technological sabotage could very well become a part of litigation strategy. Misunderstanding or tampering with VR data could lead to false interpretation, wrongly influencing the judgement. This necessitates robust security measures to shield the VR tech deployed in courtrooms.

### An Unbiased Jury: A Dream or Reality?

One of the pillars of any fair trial is an unbiased jury. However, VR might significantly influence their neutrality. Coming face-to-face with an immersive, emotional, and sometimes, graphic reproduction of criminal activity might play upon a jury's emotions, leading to decisions made on emotional grounds rather than factual evaluation.

Therefore, the question arises: How do we ensure the impartiality of the jury while simultaneously using VR to present a comprehensive perspective?

### The Future of VR in Trials: An Uncertain Trajectory

Standing on the precipice of this new frontier, it's clear that VR redefines the conduct of trials in ways previously unpredicted. As we move forward, we need to tread carefully, grappling with not only the promising prospects it offers but also addressing the challenges it poses.

The legal domain will need to come together with technological experts, legislators and society at large to build an ethical, economical, and fair framework for integrating VR into courtrooms. A framework that warrants objectivity yet takes full advantage of technology.

In the years to come, Virtual Reality will unquestionably carve out a niche for itself in the courtroom. As we stand on this precipice, the path ahead appears uncertain, challenging yet thrilling in its potential. Virtual Reality's future in courtrooms, like any disruptive technology, is about balance. It's about optimizing benefits while minimizing adverse consequences. The emphasis should be on the pursuit of justice, which, under no circumstance, should take a back seat.

This conjuncture prompts further research, public understanding, and legislative guidance. What we need is a dialogue that not only explores VR's potentials but scrutinizes its implications on the integrity of the trial process and legal values. It won't be easy, and it won't happen overnight. But if navigated effectively, the courtroom of tomorrow promises an era of unprecedented accuracy, transparency, and fairness.

As trials gradually transform into technologically enriched sessions, it's exciting, if not daunting, to imagine the courthouse of the future - one where virtual reality becomes real. As the gavel drops in the digital world, it echoes and reshapes not just our courts, but justice delivery as we know it.

www.ingramcontent.com/pod-product-compliance
Lightning Source LLC
Chambersburg PA
CBHW072221290526
45794CB00007B/2831